Tudor Theatre

Alan Childs

HODDER
Wayland

Editor: Kay Barnham
Designer: Simon Borrough
Cartoon artwork: Richard Hook
Picture research: Shelley Noronha – Glass Onion Pictures

First published in Great Britain in 2002 by Hodder Wayland, an imprint of Hodder Children's Books
© Copyright 2002 Hodder Wayland

British Library Cataloguing in Publication Data
    The history detective investigates Tudor theatre
    1. Theatre - England - History - 16th century
    2. England - Social life and customs - 16th century
    I. Title II. Tudor theatre
    792' .0942'09031

ISBN 0 7502 3738 4

Hodder Children's Books
A division of Hodder Headline Limited
338 Euston Road, London NW1 3BH

Printed and bound in Hong Kong

Picture acknowledgements:
The publishers would like to thank the following for permission to reproduce their pictures: Board of Trustees of the Armouries *cover* (bottom-left); The Bridgeman Art Library 4, 7 (bottom-right), 8 (right), 12 (top), 16, 17 (bottom), 19 (top), 21 (bottom), 22 (bottom-right); British Library 6; Corpus Christi College, Cambridge *cover* (Marlowe); Fotomas Index *cover* (left); Fine Art Photographic Library *cover* (bottom); GGS Photographics 22 (candles etc.); Kippa Matthews 5; Mary Evans Picture Library 15 (right), 21 (top); Museum of London 12 (bottom), 27 (coin); National Portrait Gallery *cover* (middle), 20 (top-left); National Youth Music Theatre 11 (left) Kenn Jacet, 11 (right) John Crook; Peter Newark's Pictures 7 (top), 10 (bottom-left), 25 (bottom), 26 (top-left), 29 (right); Ronald Grant Archive 19 (bottom); Shakespeare's Globe 1, 15 (top) Donald Cooper, 8 (left), 17 (top), 20 (bottom) John Tramper, 24 (both) Richard Kalina, 27 (bottom) Tiffany Foster; Theartarchive 28; Wayland Picture Library *cover* (right, bottom-right, bottom), 9, 10 (right), 13, 14, 18, 22 (middle), 23, 29 (left).

Contents

Did the Tudors invent acting?

*T*he Tudors loved to perform and watch plays, but they didn't invent acting. This probably happened in prehistoric times. The Greeks and Romans had open-air theatres centuries before the Tudors – our word 'theatre' even comes from a Greek word for 'seeing place'. However, acting was very popular in Tudor times (1485-1603), when important changes took place to make theatre what it is today.

Since 1264, many English towns had celebrated the festival of *Corpus Christi* with mystery or miracle plays. These were based on the lives of saints or on stories from the Bible.

This painting shows a 'booth' (tent) stage in a market square.

The history detective, Sherlock Bones, will help you to find clues and collect evidence about Tudor theatre - what theatres were like, who wrote the plays and who acted in them.

Wherever you see one of Sherlock's paw-prints, like this, you will find a mystery to solve. The answers can be found on pages 30 and 31.

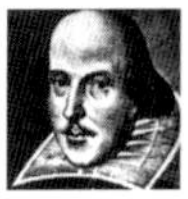

At first, simple plays were performed in churches, but when more space was needed, they spilled out on to the streets and squares. Plays were acted on small stages, or on wagons called pageants, which were pulled around the town. Sometimes the space underneath was used for changing. Everyone in the town either watched or acted – it was just like a modern carnival.

From the miracle play of 'Noah's Flood'.

Noah *Now in God's name I will begin*
To make the ship we shall go in,
When all the Earth,
through man's foul sin,
Shall lie beneath the flood.

[All, with the exception of Noah's wife, go through the motions of building the ark with various tools]

These boards I join together here
Shall bear us when the rains appear;
Then we shall sail both far and near
And safe be from the flood.

(Alexander Franklin, Seven Miracle Plays, OUP, 1963)

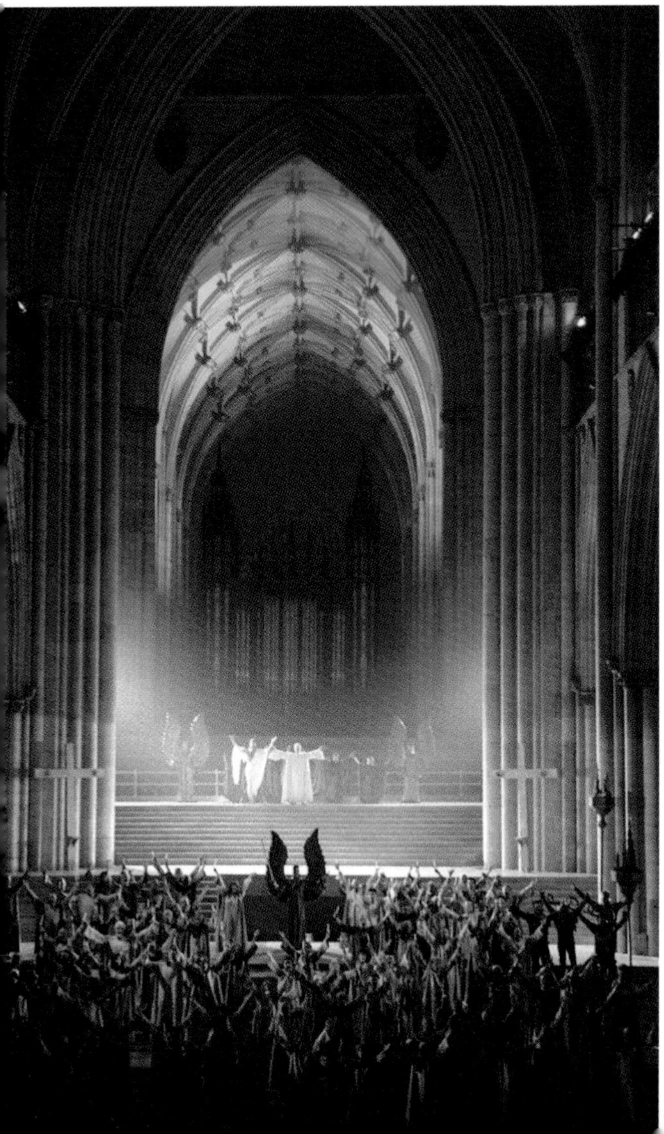

In each town, there was competition between groups of workers in craft guilds to present the best play. The plays often fitted their trade, so the Bakers' Guild might act the story of the Last Supper, and the Shipwrights the story of Noah's Ark. In York, Coventry, Chester and Wakefield, these plays have survived; they are sometimes still performed!

- Why might the Bakers' Guild be chosen to act out the story of the Last Supper?

- How might our word 'pageant' be linked to the Tudor 'pageant wagon'?

This photo shows a modern miracle play being performed in York Minster.

Detective work

Benjamin Britten's musical, *Noye's Fludde*, is based on a Chester miracle play. Ask your teacher to play part of a recording to your class. Listen out for the part when the animals go on board the ark.

What were inn-yard theatres?

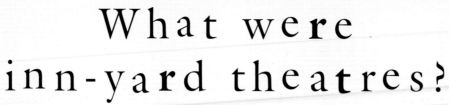

In the summer, Queen Elizabeth I (1558-1603) left hot, smelly, plague-ridden London for the countryside. Groups of actors did exactly the same thing. They set up their wagons in town squares, where they performed plays, often comedies. But audiences usually disappeared when the collecting hat was passed round. Actors staying in local inns soon realised that inn-yards made even better – and much more profitable – theatres.

Actors built their stage in the inn's courtyard, and the audience stood all around. Guests staying at the inn had a bird's-eye view from the galleries around the yard – and they were under cover too. Actors could also make sure that everyone paid, by charging the audience as they arrived.

Queen Elizabeth loved being seen when she travelled around the country.

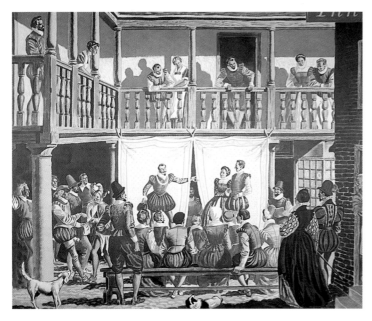

A simple stage was set up in an inn yard with the audience all around.

The audience could order beer, ale and roast beef from the inn and the innkeeper would be very pleased to have the extra trade. Some London innkeepers discovered that plays made more money than their normal trade. Like many other inns, the *Boar's Head* in Whitechapel soon became a full-time theatre. As audiences became more choosy about what they would watch, plays soon began to improve.

🐾 Which people in the inn yard do you think had the best view of the play?

Beer was served in large pewter or silver tankards.

A famous Tudor actor called Edward Alleyn (1566-1626) was often on the move. But he found ways of keeping in touch with his wife while he was touring:

I have sent you by this bearer, Thomas Pope's kinsman, my white waistcoat, because it is a trouble to me to carry it. Receive it with this letter, and lay it up for me till I come. If you send any more letters, send to me by the carriers of Shrewsbury or to West Chester or to York, to be kept till my Lord Strange's Players come.

(Henslowe Papers, ed. Walter W Greg, 1907)

🐾 How did Tudor actors like Edward Alleyn send and receive their letters?

Could anyone be an actor?

In Tudor times, anyone could become an actor – as long as they were male! Acting was not thought to be a ladylike job. If a boy's voice had not broken, he dressed up in long skirts, wore face paint and played the female roles. But women and girls had to stay in the audience…

This 'lady' in Shakespeare's *Antony and Cleopatra* is not what she seems!

DETECTIVE WORK

Are there any companies of actors performing in your area? Contact them and ask if someone could talk to your class about their work. Do they perform Shakespeare's plays or any other plays from Tudor times?

The Tudor authorities did not like actors and treated them as badly as 'rogues, vagabonds and sturdy beggars'. Parliament passed a law in 1572, which said that all actors' groups must have a licence permitting them to act. They must also have a lord as their supporter.

A carpenter called James Burbage was desperate to act, so he started a company that became *The Chamberlain's Men*. Their rich supporter, the Lord Chamberlain, was in charge of all play acting. It was lucky for actors that Queen Elizabeth I and her courtiers liked to watch plays. For a time, there was even a company acting under Elizabeth's name – the Queen's Men.

Thomas Towne, an actor with the Lord Admiral's men got deeply into debt with his theatre owner, Philip Henslowe.

Sold unto Thomas Towne, player,
a Black cloth cloak layed (covered) with silk lace
For xxvi^s viii^d to be payed by xii^d a week
and to begin payment the 2 of January 1597
and to continue weekly payment.
As lent unto Thomas Towne the 20 of March
1598 Ready money $\Big\}$ *xii^d*
Lent unto Thomas Towne (too) vpon a scarf. v^s

Henslowe's Diary, ed. Walter W Greg (Bullen 1904)

'Queen Bess' loved watching plays. Actors often performed at court.

❧ How much, in pounds (£), shillings (s) and pence (d) was Thomas Towne's black cloak? How much was he going to pay Mr Henslowe each week?

❧ Did Thomas Towne borrow any other money from Mr Henslowe?

Adult actors were paid wages or, like Shakespeare, might become a sharer in the company. Boys were taken on as apprentices to learn how to act. Some theatre owners made sure that their actors stayed with them by lending them money, often to buy expensive costumes – it could take months to pay off the loan. Other owners made their actors sign up for a number of years before they would let them join their company.

Who were the youngest actors?

Even rich children had few books at home or at school, so they learnt lessons by heart and acted out well-known stories like *Beauty and the Beast* or *Tom Thumb*. During the long Christmas celebrations, boys and even girls joined in the masked mummers' plays. But, grammar school pupils had a much harder job – the plays they performed in front of their friends were in Latin…

In London, richer boys who went to choir schools, such as St Paul's and the Chapel Royal, were given the chance to act. There were no adults in their companies, and the audience paid to see them. Often the boys performed before Elizabeth I!

St Paul's Cathedral had a small playhouse used by the choir school boys.

The boy actors attending this wedding feast could be very cold!

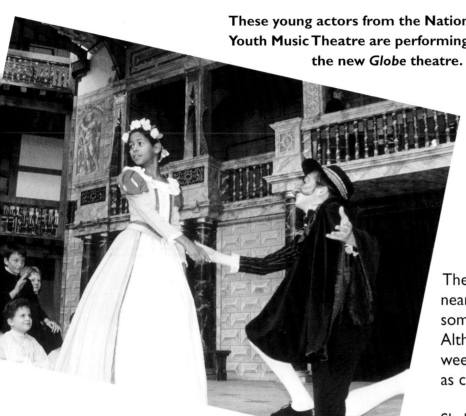

These young actors from the National Youth Music Theatre are performing at the new *Globe* theatre.

The *Paul's Children* acted in a small theatre near the cathedral. It was hard work and sometimes the boys were treated cruelly. Although they only performed once a week, they had to attend lessons as well as countless rehearsals.

Shakespeare teased the boy actors in his play *Hamlet*. One of the characters calls them 'little eyases' (singing birds). A famous boy actor called Salomon Pavey was brilliant at playing old men. Sadly he died when he was only 13 years old, probably from the plague.

> *Weep with me, all you that read*
> *This little story;*
> *And know, for whom a tear you shed*
> *Death's self is sorry.*
> *'Twas a child that so did thrive*
> *In grace and feature,*
> *As Heaven and Nature seem'd to strive*
> *Which owned the creature.*
> *Years he numbered scarce thirteen*
> *When Fates turn'd cruel,*
> *Yet three filled Zodiacs had he been*
> *The stage's jewel;*
> *And did act (what now we moan)*
> *Old men so duly*
> *As sooth the Parcae (Fates) thought him one,*
> *He played so truly.*
>
> (Ben Jonson, Epitaph for Salomon Pavey –
> a child of the Chapel Royal, 1602)

DETECTIVE WORK

Try to find out about any drama groups for young people in your area, and also about the *National Youth Music Theatre*. One of their productions is called *Salomon Pavey*, named after the young Tudor actor.

🐾 In the poem on the left Ben Jonson is saying that the 'Fates' killed 13-year-old Salomon Pavey accidentally. Read the last four lines of this extract and work out why.

When were
new theatres built?

*I*n 1576, the carpenter-turned-actor, James Burbage, built one of the first playhouses in London. It was simply called the *Theatre*. He built it north of London's city walls because, inside the city, the Lord Mayor often stopped all play-acting with the smallest excuse.

Burbage had a deadly rival, a businessman called Philip Henslowe. He had run a theatre and bear-baiting contests, but now he also wanted a brand-new theatre of his own. In 1587, he built the *Rose* south of the River Thames in Southwark, another area outside the Lord Mayor's control.

At bear-baiting contests, a chained bear was attacked and tormented by fierce dogs.

DETECTIVE WORK

Find picture maps of Tudor London and look at the areas where theatres were built. Compare the maps with a map of modern London, looking for the same areas and any buildings or streets that still exist.

The *Globe* and the *Rose* were built in Southwark, south of the Thames.

Soon after James Burbage died, his sons quarrelled with the landlord of the *Theatre* and decided to pull the building down. They used the parts to build the *Globe* in 1599. As the Burbages' theatre was very near the *Rose*, Henslowe ordered yet another new theatre to be built at once, north of the city walls. The theatre was called the *Fortune* and Henslowe wanted it to be even bigger than the *Globe*...

The original *Fortune* was burnt down in 1621 and rebuilt in brick.

🐾 Why do you think Philip Henslowe wanted the *Fortune* theatre to be bigger than the *Globe*?

🐾 Why would rebuilding a Tudor theatre be easier than rebuilding a modern building?

This is a contract made between Philip Henslowe and the carpenter Peter Street, to build the *Fortune* theatre.

(The carpenter shall) provide and find all manner of workmen, timber, joists, rafters, boards, doors, bolts, hinges, brick, tile, lathe, lime, hair, sand, nails, lead, iron, glass, workmanship and other things whatsoever... and shall also make all the said frame in every point for scantlings (dimensions) larger and bigger in assize (size) than the scantlings of the timber of the said new erected house called the Globe.

('Henslowe Papers', ed. Walter W Greg, Bullen, 1907)

What were theatres like?

Tudor theatres were not very comfortable. Most of them were open to the sky, so if it rained some of the audience got wet. Shakespeare called the *Globe* a 'wooden O'. From a distance the building looked round, but it may have had twenty sides.

This drawing of the *Swan* theatre is the only one which shows what a Tudor theatre looked like inside.

❧ On a tracing, draw lines down from the corners of the stage, then across to the bottom of the strange pillars – are these really pillars, or gaps in a curtain?

❧ How good is your Latin? Look for these words on the *Swan* drawing and see if you can match them with their English meanings.

porticus	stage
tectum	benches
mimorum aedes	seats for wealthy
planities sive arena	roof
orchestra	actors' dressing room
ingressus	covered gallery
proscaenium	entrance to steps
sedilia	the yard

The new *Globe* theatre presents plays just as the Tudors did.

DETECTIVE WORK

Find out if there are any theatres nearby that do *not* have a normal 'picture-frame' stage. Does the audience sit round the stage? Are there balconies for spectators? Although it is not open-air, the *Maddermarket Theatre* in Norwich is based on the design of a Tudor theatre.

Inside the theatre, the stage jutted out into the yard, or 'pit', and the audience stood all around it. Richer customers sat in galleries around the yard, as they did in inn-yard theatres. During the performance food and drink was carried round the audience.

Above the stage was a roof, held up by two pillars, and at the top was a little 'hut'. The ceiling beneath the roof often had stars and clouds painted on it – this was nicknamed the 'heavens'. Everything near the stage was brightly painted too.

A walking Tudor drinks dispenser!

In 1594, the *Swan* theatre was built in Southwark, not far from the *Rose*.

Of all the theatres, however, the largest and most distinguished is that wherof the sign is a swan (commonly called the Swan *theatre) since it has space for three thousand persons, and is built of a concrete of flint stones (which greatly abound in Britain) and supported by wooden columns, painted in such excellent imitation of marble that it might deceive even the most prying.*

(Copy of letter by Johannes de Witt, c1596, University Library, Utrecht)

There was usually a small curtained area at the back of the stage, which could become a cave or a bed-chamber. Above this was a balcony, very useful in a play such as *Romeo and Juliet*.

The actors 'attired' (dressed) themselves in the 'tiring house' behind the stage, helped by the 'tireman'. He also kept one eye on the 'platt' (plot), which was nailed up by the door, to make sure nothing was forgotten.

Were there special effects?

Although special effects in Tudor times were not as breathtaking as today, there were plenty of surprises for Tudor audiences. A swordsman might thrust his weapon into a hidden pig's bladder and his enemy would bleed real blood...

Some of the special effects were created in the 'hut' up above the stage. A wooden winch with a rope was used to lower a 'God' on his 'creaking throne'. He would appear through a trapdoor in the painted ceiling of the roof. In a play called *Cymbeline*, Shakespeare's instructions are:

'Jupiter descends in thunder and lightning, sitting upon an eagle; he throws a thunderbolt; the Ghosts fall on their knees.'

There indeed a man may behold shaggy-haired devils run roaring over the stage with squibs in their mouths, while drummers make thunder in the tiring house, and the twelve penny hirelings make artificial lightning in their heavens.

(John Milton, Astrologaster, 1620)

❧ What would we call the things the 'shaggy-haired devils' had in their mouths?

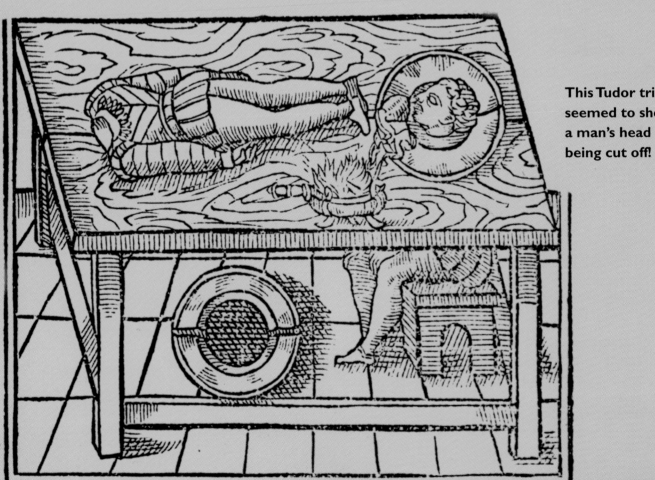

This Tudor trick seemed to show a man's head being cut off!

A stage trapdoor is being used in this scene from Shakespeare's *Hamlet*.

DETECTIVE WORK

Find out about stagecraft in your school or local library. How do people 'fly' across the stage? How are special effects that were impossible in Shakespeare's time created today?

The Tudors loved lots of noise in their battle scenes. Sometimes cannon were fired in the fields around the theatre or fireworks set alight in the hut and run along strings down to the stage. The sound of thunder was made by a drum, or by rolling around real cannon balls in a box called the 'cannon-ball run'.

Even the space beneath the stage could be used for special effects. Imagine how scared the audience would be when a white-faced ghost appeared from a trapdoor in the centre of the stage…

This painting shows extravagant scenery made for a Tudor play.

Who went to the theatre?

*I*f the theatre flag was flying, everyone knew that a performance would take place that day. When the trumpet blew at two o'clock, the excited audience hurried across London Bridge, or urged watermen to row their water taxis even faster. The show was about to begin!

Tudor play-goers wait to pay their penny to the 'gatherer'.

Just like today, if you paid more, you got a better seat in the audience. Poorer people, the 'groundlings', paid a penny to the 'gatherer' to stand by the stage. Richer people were charged another penny or two for a seat in one of the galleries. The wooden benches were hard, and a cushion cost *another* penny. The very richest might hire a room near the stage for sixpence, to be well away from the poor – they might even sit on a stool to the side of the stage.

Almost every type of person went to the theatre, from the very wealthy to young apprentices who could scarcely afford the penny admission. There were law students, market-women, shopkeepers, soldiers home from war… and criminals. Plays were often noisy and while the audience joined in, cutpurses and pickpockets did their work.

There were plenty of refreshments to choose from – the audience could buy beer and ale, pippins (apples) and pears, nuts and ginger-bread. Toilet facilities, or 'jakes', were very basic – the nearest toilet was the River Thames!

Small boats could be hired to cross the river to the theatres.

DETECTIVE WORK

Ask your teacher if your class can watch an old film called *Henry V*, starring Laurence Olivier. The opening shot shows a view of Tudor London, followed by the first scenes of a play at the *Globe*. Look carefully at the audience, and watch for a pair of Tudor spectacles.

Laurence Olivier starred as the king in the 1944 film of Shakespeare's *Henry V*.

✿ Look at the picture of the River Thames at the top of this page. What was unusual about old London Bridge?

Who was Will Shakespeare?

William Shakespeare was probably the most famous playwright of all time, but a great deal of his life remains a mystery. We know that he was born in Stratford in 1564, and that his father was a wealthy merchant. But we don't know why he decided to become an actor. Perhaps he saw James Burbage's company, or watched the mystery plays in nearby Coventry.

Young Will set out for London to make his fortune, and joined Burbage's company of actors. His first job was looking after the horses at the theatre, but he soon started to act small roles. Then his great gift of writing was discovered and he became a 'sharer' in the company, helping to run it.

Will Shakespeare worked at the *Globe* and wrote many of his plays for that theatre. He made the audience imagine the things he could not bring on to the stage:

This is probably a portrait of Shakespeare. Can you see his one gold earring?

DETECTIVE WORK

Are there any Shakespeare plays being performed in your area? When was the play written?

Look up Shakespeare and Stratford on the Internet to find out more about the great playwright and his place of birth.

Think when we talk of horses that you see them Printing their proud hooves i' the receiving earth.

🐾 What was the name of the large house Shakespeare bought in Stratford? Use the Internet or reference books to help you.

🐾 Shakespeare died on a special day of the year. What day was it?

Shakespeare's plays are still performed at the new *Globe* theatre. These actors are in a production of *Hamlet*.

This is the house in Stratford where Shakespeare was born.

He knew what his audience liked, and wrote comic scenes that would make them laugh. They were sometimes written specially for comic actors like Will Kemp.

When Will Shakespeare finally returned to Stratford, he lived in one of the biggest houses there. He died on 23 April 1616.

This painting shows Shakespeare with a group of friends, including playwright Ben Jonson, poet John Donne and Elizabethan adventurer, Sir Walter Raleigh.

Shakespeare's works	
1590	Henry VI, Part 1
	Henry VI, Part 2
	Henry VI, part 3
1592	Richard III
	Titus Andronicus
1593	The Comedy of Errors
	The Taming of the Shrew
1594	The Two Gentlemen of Verona
	Love's Labour's Lost
1595	Romeo and Juliet
	Richard II
1596	A Midsummer Night's Dream
	King John
1597	The Merchant of Venice
	Henry IV, Part 1
1598	Henry IV, Part 2
	The Merry Wives of Windsor
1599	Henry V
	Much Ado About Nothing
	Julius Caesar
1600	As You Like It
	Twelfth Night
1601	Hamlet
1602	Troilus and Cressida
1603	All's Well That Ends Well
	Measure for Measure
1604	Othello
1605	Timon of Athens
1606	King Lear
	Macbeth
1607	Antony and Cleopatra
	Coriolanus
1608	Pericles
1609	Cymbeline
	(Sonnets published)
1610	A Winter's Tale
1611	The Tempest
1612	Henry VIII

Were all theatres open-air?

London had both indoor and open-air theatres. For many years before the Tudors, plays had been performed inside the great halls of large country houses, for weddings or at Christmas. There was often a wooden screen in these halls, with doors on either side and a balcony above. It is possible that this was copied in open-air theatres.

Indoor theatres were much smaller than open-air theatres and there was no standing area. The prices for admission were very high – as much as sixpence for the cheapest ticket – and it was often too expensive for ordinary people to attend. The very best seats, near or on the stage, could cost half a crown (30 old pence).

Candles were used to light indoor theatres, which could become very smoky.

Halls in large country houses were like the first indoor theatres.

Travelling actors with masks and instruments entertained rich guests.

Indoor theatres were useful in wintertime, or during bad weather. Burbage's company used the second *Blackfriar's Theatre* as well as the *Globe*, moving plays from one theatre to the other.

Actors were also asked to perform their plays at Queen Elizabeth's palaces, such as Whitehall. The companies would audition before the Master of the Revels – the Queen's special adviser for plays and masques. No expense was spared for costumes or scenery.

DETECTIVE WORK

Find out more about Tudor masques from reference books. Perform an entertainment before the 'Queen', with musicians, dancers, and an audience.

Masques were special entertainments with rich costumes, music and dancing.

I saw the children of Paul's last night…
I' faith I like the audience that frequenteth there
With much applause: A man shall not be choked
With the stench of garlic, not be pasted
To the barmy jacket of a beer brewer…
'Tis a good gentle audience.

(John Marston, Jack Drum's Entertainment, 1600)

In John Marston's play, why do you think the speaker preferred the kind of audience he found in St Paul's indoor theatre?

What did he say the 'groundlings' smelled of in the open-air theatres?

How were theatres built?

*I*n the dead of night on 28 December 1598, there were strange goings-on around the Burbages' *Theatre*. A group of 'conspirators' met the actor Richard Burbage, and the carpenter Peter Street, and they started pulling down the whole building. The timbers were then taken across London Bridge over the frozen River Thames to be rebuilt on the other side as the *Globe*. And this was all because of a quarrel with their landlord!

The framework of Tudor buildings was made in the carpenter's yard, then the numbered sections taken to the site. Young 'green' oak was used, which locked together as it dried. Wooden pegs held the joints securely. Foundation trenches were filled with 'clunch' (crushed limestone), then a brick base wall was built for the timber building to sit on.

The new Globe used Norfolk reeds – the first London thatch since 1666.

Once the building's frame was erected, upright staves and thin horizontal strips of wood called laths filled the gaps. These were covered with plaster made from sand, lime and cow's hair. Finally, the roof was thatched with reeds.

In Shakespeare's original *Globe*, the beams would probably have been plastered over.

✿ Why was thatch no longer used for roofs after 1666?

DETECTIVE WORK

Are there any old Tudor houses in your area? Try to visit one, and look at how it was built. Look especially for the wooden pegs, the laths and plaster, and the smaller Tudor bricks. Remember to take your cameras.

The area where the audience stood often became muddy. Ash, sand and crushed hazelnut shells were spread out to help drainage, and to make a soft surface to stand on.

The biggest danger with all these materials was fire, and in 1613 the first *Globe* went up in flames. Luckily, 3,000 people escaped, although one man's breeches caught light. He was saved when someone threw a bottle of ale over him!

✤ Why do you think the audience at the *Globe* failed to notice that a fire had started?

Tudor builders learnt from their mistakes. When the second *Globe* was built in 1613 after the fire, they used tiles instead of thatch for the roof.

> *The King's Players had a new play (Henry VIII)… and certain cannons being shot off… some of the paper, or other stuff, wherewith one of them was stopped, did light on the thatch, where being thought at first but an idle smoke, and their eyes more attentive to the show, it kindled inwardly and ran round like a train (trail of gunpowder), consuming within less than an hour the whole house to the very ground.*
>
> (Henry Wotton – letter to Edmund Bacon, Reliquiae Wottoniae, 1685)

How does archaeology help?

Archaeologists have to search through centuries of buildings to uncover a site.

By strange coincidence, the sites of the old *Rose* theatre and the *Globe* were discovered within a few months of each other, in 1988-9. Archaeologists were very excited because this was their first chance to explore the remains of not one, but *two* Tudor theatres. They hoped that the digs would tell them whether earlier guesses that had been made about the two theatres were correct...

Archaeologists can encounter many problems when digging in an old city like London. Layers of history have to be carefully removed. Of the two theatres, it was much easier to uncover the remains of the *Rose*. The foundations of the *Globe* were buried underneath a main road and some houses.

At the end of their lives, both theatres had been taken down, but their foundations revealed lots of evidence. At the *Globe*, for example, archaeologists found a stair turret (extra outside stairway). This showed that in later times rich people probably did not go through the smelly yard to get to the galleries. At the *Rose*, the entrance door seemed to be very narrow. This could have been to help the 'gatherer' to prevent cheating. If people came through the entrance one at a time, it would be easier to charge them.

✿ Why is it difficult for archaeologists to work in a city like London?

DETECTIVE WORK

The *Globe's* website can be found at *http://www.shakespeares-globe.org/* – learn as much as you can about how the new theatre was built. Even better, plan a class visit.

Tudor Maths: ask your teacher to show you how the angles of the outside walls would show archaeologists how many sides each theatre had.

When some of the outside walls of the *Globe* were uncovered, they measured exactly 16.5 feet (just over five metres), the same length as the Tudor measurement called a 'rod'. Then, when two adjoining sections of wall were found, the angle could be seen. This evidence told the archaeologists what size and shape to build the new *Globe*.

A coin found in the *Rose* theatre.

This photo shows the new *Globe* theatre under construction.

A name of the Rose asks for time

As archaeologists were pleading for more time to investigate the Elizabethan Rose Playhouse they believe they have found at Bankside, Southwark, South London, the... descendant of the man who built it, Mr Philip Henslowe, joined the campaign. Mr Henslowe... said: 'It is a key link with the theatre of our ancestors...' Mr C Walter Hodges, a theatre historian, said the find was the most important clue to Tudor entertainment since a drawing of the Swan Theatre... was found in 1888.

The Times, 15 February 1989

Your project

Topic Questions
1. What ideas did Tudor theatres copy from the inn-yard theatres?
2. Can you describe a year in the life of a Tudor actor?
3. What do we know about child actors in Tudor times?
4. What would it have been like to visit a Tudor theatre?
5. How much do we know about William Shakespeare?

Project presentation

1. Design a Tudor poster advertising a play. Discuss what information is needed on the poster, and how you will attract an audience.

2. Imagine that you are a Tudor boy or girl visiting the *Globe*. Write a diary of your experiences – you could even use a quill pen!

3. Make a cut-away model of part of a Tudor open-air theatre, using the information in this book. A large box without top or bottom, opened out, can be scored and folded to make the shapes of the sides; the thatched roof and galleries can be painted on. This should be glued to a baseboard. The stage and the hut can then be made separately and glued on. You could make peg-doll (or pipe-cleaner) figures for the actors and audience.

4. Imagine that radio had been invented in Tudor times. Take your microphone to a Tudor theatre and interview the owner, or the actors, or perhaps even Will Shakespeare himself. Work out the questions carefully, and make sure that the classmates you are interviewing know what they are going to talk about.

Kemps nine daies wonder.
Performed in a daunce from
London to Norwich.

When Will Kemp left Shakespeare's company he decided to dance from Norwich to London as a publicity stunt.

5. In drama, make up a play about taking down the old *Theatre* secretly at night, and moving the timbers across London Bridge to build the *Globe*. The landlord and his men might try to stop you!

Richard Tarlton was Elizabeth's jester and one of the most famous Tudor comic actors.

Sherlock Bones has been finding out about a famous comic actor in Shakespeare's time called Richard Tarlton, who used a dog in his act. It is said that Tarlton had only to put his head round the door to make the audience laugh. He wore country clothes with a buttoned cap, and carried a pipe and tabor (drum). When Tarlton died, his book of jokes was published.

Sherlock Bones has discovered that Shakespeare may have based a character in one of his plays on Richard Tarlton. Can you help Sherlock to do his project by looking up a play called *The Two Gentleman of Verona*: Act II, Scene III? Sherlock would like to know the dog's name in the play, and his owner's name. He would also like to know why the owner is annoyed with the dog.

Shakespeare's friends made sure that his plays were published for future generations.

> *Tarlton when his head was only seen,*
> *The Tirehouse door and Tapestry between*
> *Set all the multitude in such a laughter*
> *They could not hold for scarce an hour after.*
>
> (Henry Peacham, Thalia's Banquet, 1620)

Glossary

apprentices Young boys learning a trade.

carrier A man with a delivery cart

Corpus Christi A church festival.

craft guilds A group of workmen in the same trade.

galleries Covered seating areas.

groundlings The audience standing around the stage.

heavens The upper parts of a Tudor open-air theatre.

masque An entertainment with music and dancing

Master of the Revels The Queen's official who checked plays.

mummers Medieval plays performed in mime.

pageant A wagon stage.

pewter A metal made of a mixture of tin, copper and lead.

platt The outline of the play.

poaching Stealing, usually animals.

rod A Tudor measurement – just over five metres.

sharer An important actor who had shares in the company.

tiring house Where the actors changed.

vagabonds Rascals; homeless people.

watermen The river boatmen, who took passengers.

Answers

page 5: 🐾 The Last Supper was when Jesus shared a meal of *bread* and wine with his disciples.

🐾 A pageant today can mean a grand performance, or procession. Pageant waggons in Tudor times were also used in processions, and for acting plays on.

page 7: 🐾 Probably the people in the gallery would see best, with their high viewpoint and no one in front of them.

🐾 Letters would be sent by carriers' horses and carts, which travelled between towns with goods and people.

page 8: 🐾 In old money, there were 20 shillings in a pound and 12 pence in a shilling. The cloak cost 26 shillings and eight pence – or one pound, six shillings and eight pence. His repayment was 12 pence a week.

🐾 He also borrowed 'ready money' and five shillings for a scarf.

page 11: 🐾 Ben Jonson is saying that Salomon was so good at playing old men that the Fates caused him to die, thinking he really *was* old.

page 13: 🐾 Because he wanted to 'score a point' against his deadly rivals, the Burbage family, or because he wanted more seats and therefore more profit.

🐾 It was easier to rebuild a Tudor building because it was made of timber. The sections could be taken apart and then put together again.

page 14: 🐾
porticus – covered gallery
tectum – roof
mimorum aedes – actors' dressing room
planities sive arena – the yard
orchestra – seats for the wealthy
ingressus – entrance to steps
proscaenium – stage
sedilia – benches.

page 14: ✿ no one really knows, but the strange sketchy shape of the pillars and the thin stage may suggest that they are dark gaps in the curtain.

page 16: ✿ fireworks.

page 19: ✿ There were houses along the bridge.

page 20: ✿ It was called New Place.

✿ He died on St George's Day (the patron saint of England).

page 23: ✿ He preferred this audience because they were richer – and less smelly! He said that the groundlings smelt of garlic.

page 24: ✿ The Fire of London happened in 1666. After this date thatch was not allowed.

page 25: ✿ They were concentrating on the play, or they might have thought it was part of the special effects.

page 26: ✿ Over the centuries, many houses have been built, so layers of history have to be carefully removed.

Books to read

Stories of Tudor Times (Master Will's New Theatre) by Alan Childs (Anglia Young Books, 1995)

Look Inside a Shakespearian Theatre, by Peter Chrisp (Wayland, 1998)

Shakespeare: A Life, by Wendy Greenhill and Paul Wignall (Heinmann, 1996)

Shakespeare's Theatre, by Andrew Langley (OUP, 1999)

Cue for Treason, by Geoffrey Trease (Puffin, 1965)

King of Shadows (for older readers), by Susan Cooper (The Bodley Head, 1999)

Index

Numbers in **bold** refer to pictures and captions